Releasing Anger

About the pamphlet
Anger is a feeling, like happiness, which is natural to all people. In this pamphlet the author illustrates how anger can sometimes endanger recovery and how, properly understood, it can also enhance serenity and self-knowledge.

Hazelden Classics for Clients

Releasing Anger

Richard S.

HAZELDEN

Hazelden
Center City, Minnesota 55012-0176

1-800-328-9000
1-651-213-4590 (Fax)
www.hazelden.org

Any stories or case studies that may be used in this material are composites of many individuals. Names and details have been changed to protect identities.

ISBN-13: 978-0-89486-249-6
ISBN-10: 0-89486-249-9

Cover and interior design by David Spohn
Typesetting by Tursso Companies

INTRODUCTION

Many of us in Twelve Step programs find anger difficult to express in a direct and healthy manner, and consequently it becomes a key issue in recovery. Even those nonalcoholics who were raised in alcoholic families have often responded to their situation with rage, blaming, resentment, guilt, and even physical abuse as a result of repressed anger. Many of us have learned to avoid any expression that even remotely suggests anger in order to "keep the peace." This anger inevitably becomes cold and resentful. Resentment can quickly undermine any growth a person attains in a Twelve Step program and will ultimately threaten sobriety. This pamphlet will show ways to apply the principles of the Twelve Steps to help us express our anger directly. We'll see how denial of anger, not the feeling itself, is what undermines our relationships and serenity. We can choose to deny our anger or express it. We needn't continue old behavior.

Anger isn't a demon to be exorcised from our bodies, or an unwelcome guest to be thrown out of our house of feeling. Anger is not a "bad feeling," but a normal and healthy one. Everyone has felt and will continue to feel anger from time to time. Being in touch with our feelings doesn't mean we will never experience discomfort. Often, in fact, awareness of feelings puts us directly in touch with what bothers, hurts, or angers us. We need to get in touch with and become more aware of our anger.

In this pamphlet we'll discuss questions we can ask ourselves that will make our feelings more clear. We'll rehearse techniques to release our anger, review situations that frequently anger and irritate us, and find methods of dealing with anger we can use to bring more comfort and emotional balance to our lives.

DENYING ANGER

When we are genuinely happy, our bodies cannot help but express our feelings. Our eyes glow, our limbs seem weightless, our muscles relax, and we smile. Sadness brings a downturned mouth, drooping facial muscles, slumping shoulders, and sometimes tears. Anger is no different. It has its own physiology.

We can see and hear anger. Capillaries fill with blood that color the face; the volume of the voice rises; words are pronounced emphatically; arms and hands grow firm and tense; gestures are more pronounced; blood pressure goes up. These are only a few of the body's physiological responses to anger.

Others will often see and hear our anger long before we recognize it. When our anger is clear to others and they ask us how we feel, sometimes we say, "No, I'm not angry." This is *denial*. When we lie about what we feel, eventually we disown the feeling, and anger is usually not the only feeling we deny. The severity of our denial of anger is always proportional to our denial of tender and loving feelings. The more able we are to admit, accept, and express our anger, the same will be true of our love.

Imagine a train speeding down the tracks. Someone pulls the emergency cord to stop it. We can easily imagine the reaction. People are thrown forward, luggage comes tumbling down from overhead racks, and injury may result. Everyone on the train questions the conductor and wonders what's happened. When anger arises and we try to stop our bodily responses with denial, the same havoc and destruction takes place inside us. Ulcers, backaches, colitis, high blood pressure, headaches, and grinding of the teeth are only some of the problems that can result when we suppress our anger. Why, then, do we sometimes go to any length, even to the point of becoming physically ill, to deny it? Before discussing this problem, let's take a look at someone who denies anger when, from all appearances, he or she seems to be experiencing that very feeling.

PASSIVE-AGGRESSIVE TYPES

We've often heard the term *passive-aggressive* used to describe people who feel one way but act another. When they are angry, they work very hard at looking comfortable to con us into believing they are happy. Rather than frown, they smile; rather than tense their bodies, they intentionally swing their arms and legs. Their anger isn't expressed warmly or directly. These people, more than most, suffer from feeling what they "should not" feel. Their anger, when it arises, is expressed with mild, sugar-coated remarks. They laugh inappropriately. They prefer to discuss our feelings, rather than their own. But the true anger gives their remarks an odd, aggressive quality. Sometimes we can't put our finger on it. But if we trust our feelings, we sense they are aggressive, and we feel uneasy. Occasionally, we all act this way.

Passive-aggressive people often boast about how they never get angry, as if anger wasn't simply a human feeling we all have but a disease or shortcoming of some kind. Imagine, for a moment, a passive-aggressive person (let's say it's a man) at a party, standing in a crowded living room. His spouse has just made an unkind and insensitive remark about him. This person, rather than show any feelings of hurt or anger, will often smile and say, "You shouldn't say things like that" or "You don't really mean that." And as he leans over the coffee table to pick up a snack, he changes the subject. From all appearances, he looks comfortable.

If you comment to him privately about your own feelings regarding his spouse's remark, he may well minimize or excuse it by discussing, not how *he* feels, but the stress his spouse is under at her new job. He might explain the *why* of her behavior, but will rarely discuss *how* he feels about it. He may end the conversation by thanking you for your concern and advising you not to worry about him. In truth, worry, anxiety, and depression follow these people like shadows.

Passive-aggressive people are driven to control their feelings and will deny any emotion, such as anger, that makes them feel vulnerable and powerless. They want to feel powerful and in charge. They focus on controlling the feelings and behavior of others. They may advise their children on what feelings they "should" or "shouldn't" have. They may tell their daughters that anger is unladylike, and their sons that showing pain is unmanly. Any time we use the terms *should* or *shouldn't* in regard to other people's feelings, we are participating in this passive-aggressive behavior. This same denial motivates more aggressive people.

AGGRESSIVE TYPES

The *aggressive* types tell us they always let out their anger; they have no problem, they say, in expressing it. They may yell and shake a fist, but when we examine their remarks we hear blaming and shaming. "You *make me* angry" is a characteristic remark. Rather than take responsibility for their own feelings, aggressive types often blame others for their anger. In essence, they are saying, "You are the one who made me feel this way and I want you to stop what you're doing so I can feel good." All the yelling is an attempt to control and manipulate others into acting and behaving the way the aggressive person wants. Since aggressive people can't warmly express their anger, the other people will have to change.

You might find this person at a street corner, involved in a fender-bender, yelling and accusing the other person of driving carelessly. "It's your fault; you shouldn't have stopped so quickly" or "You should have signaled your turn properly." Even if this person receives a ticket, you'll often find him or her at home, eight hours later, blaming the other driver over supper. However, we must remember that anger is neither right nor wrong, does not try to win or lose arguments, and does not find fault or excuse. If the goal of expressing our anger (or any feeling) is to show those we love who we are, then we can see how far away passive-aggressive and aggressive people are from this goal. We must also keep in mind that all of us periodically engage in passive-aggressive or aggressive behavior. We need to identify this behavior in order to share our real selves with those we love.

WHAT ANGERS US?

Suppose, for a moment, your spouse fails to pay a bill due on a particular date. Or someone arrives late for a meeting with you, or you have a flat tire, or the door handle suddenly comes off in your hands just as you are rushing out of the house to an appointment. Perhaps you don't like to be hurried or kept waiting by someone else. Many things irritate, disappoint, and anger us. It's helpful to know what specific situations trigger our anger. If we take a quick inventory of these situations and compare our list with someone else's, we'll see many similarities. This will help us realize we aren't alone. None of us likes a flat tire when we are driving to an important appointment. Most anyone can understand our being angry and irritated.

Try to include in your list some quirky situations that seem to anger only you. Maybe cigarette butts in ashtrays irritate you, and even more so the individual who left them there. Maybe your spouse seems to have a habit of calling you downstairs just as you settle down in bed to read. Do you tighten your jaws when your child cries in the middle of the night? Do you get angry and mumble under your breath when you find the shirt or blouse you wanted to wear wrinkled? Identifying these situations now, when you are more comfortable and willing to be more aware of anger, will make it easier to express your anger when the situation happens.

It's important to keep these situations in mind; the flat tire, the wrinkled shirt, the unpaid bill, showing up late for an appointment—none of these things happened intentionally to harm or anger us. The tire did not pick that moment to go flat when we so needed the car to run smoothly. In fact, we might have known all along the tire needed to be replaced. Nor did someone anticipate our desire to wear a particular shirt and sneak in, in the middle of the night, to wrinkle it. Absurd as this may sound, blaming others or the situation for our anger is just as ridiculous.

THEN WHY GET ANGRY?

Suppose we have a friend who is chronically late for appointments. While waiting at a restaurant, we find ourselves angry and irritated. When she arrives and apologizes for being late, we say, "Oh, it's all right. It doesn't bother me." We may feel we are simply being polite, but in truth we are choosing to deny our anger and keep it inside us. With each late arrival and each denial of anger, we are shaping a resentment that will damage us spiritually. "But I shouldn't be angry," we might say. "Should" or "shouldn't" have nothing to do with our feelings. Feelings simply are. "But why get angry?" we ask. "It won't change anything." The question, however, denies and avoids the obvious. We *are* angry, and the question should be rephrased: "Why express the anger?" We can choose to express or deny our feelings. Later we'll talk about how we can make that choice, but for now let's look again at ourselves waiting for our friend to show up for our lunch date.

First, we identify how we feel. Whether we should or shouldn't feel angry is beside the point. If we decide to tell her we feel angry and expect this to change her behavior, we are on the wrong track. If we share our anger and irritation with her, she may realize how we feel about her tardiness and apologize, promising to make more of an effort to arrive on time. However, this may not happen and should not be the goal. We express our feelings not to change other people, but to share with them who we are, how we feel. We express our anger to our friend because we don't want to injure ourselves—and, in the long run, her—by denying or dismissing our feelings as unimportant.

RELEASING ANGER

Awareness of our anger is half of learning to get in touch with our feelings. Many of us who spent our childhoods in alcoholic families and became alcoholics ourselves never knew what our true feelings were or how to express them in a healthy manner. The First Step can help us immeasurably to recognize and express our anger. By simply admitting we are powerless to control what, where, and when we feel angry, we deepen our awareness of the very nature of feelings. We have no more control over any feeling—mad, sad, glad, or bad—than we do over thoughts that pop in and out of our minds. How many times have we been surprised at a party, at an AA meeting, or simply on a walk by a feeling that changed a bad day into a good one? How happy we felt at unexpectedly seeing an old friend at a party? We can be surprised in the same way by anger. One minute we can be sitting comfortably in the car at a stoplight, and the next minute, a little farther up the road, feel angry that another car pulled out of a side street in front of us, causing a near-collision. We do not control these events, or the corresponding feelings we have. Instead, we admit to our powerlessness and give up trying to control others, their behavior, and situations to suit our own feelings. We admit, as well, to the unmanageability we feel when angry. This is the First Step, the beginning of awareness of our anger and its healthy expression.

The principles of the Twelve Steps teach us other ways of dealing with anger. After admitting to powerlessness and unmanageability, we can come to believe that a Power greater than ourselves can lead us to a healthy expression of our feelings, to sanity, to wholeness.

In the Third Step, we do not so much turn over our feelings to the God of our understanding but the attempts to control our feelings by denying them, by manipulating others, or by blaming. God wants us to have our feelings, to experience them fully, even anger.

Earlier we discussed an inventory of situations that often anger us. The Fourth Step can also help us inventory how, in the past, we dealt with our feelings, especially anger. We can discuss this with a close friend and admit to him or her "the exact nature of our wrongs." When we come to the Sixth and Seventh Steps, it's important we understand that anger is *not* a character defect or shortcoming; anger is a normal, human feeling. What we do or don't do with that feeling can reveal a character defect, but it is not wrong to feel angry. Denial of anger, blaming, resentment, and manipulating others are character defects or shortcomings that result from *not* dealing with our anger in a healthy way. We are willing to have God remove these defects, and we humbly ask Him to do so. We are not asking God to take our feelings, and this includes anger, out of our hearts. By now, we can return to people in our past and make amends, with feeling, for not listening to their feelings or responding honestly to them with our own.

The Tenth Step asks us to continue an inventory. This can simply entail periodic spot checks on how we feel. Asking ourselves, "How do I feel, right now?" can help us to become more aware of how subtly our feelings connect us to others and our environment. Through the prayer and meditation suggested by the Eleventh Step, we can seek advice from others and our Higher Power on how to best deal with anger. As we become more aware of our own feelings, we experience a more heightened sense of life. Just as our palate develops our taste for foods, feelings develop our taste for life. Anger helps us see what we like or don't like. And just as sobriety is the message we carry to others, so, too, expressing our feelings also carries a message. As others see and hear us express our anger warmly and openly, they, too, are encouraged to deal with their own feelings.

The Steps encourage us to take responsibility for our feelings, and help us choose what to say or do with them. Sometimes it will be necessary to seek out the other person and admit our feelings to him or her. The person we choose to express our anger to directly and openly will often be a close friend or loved one. Anger and love for another are often intertwined. Anger, as well as happiness, sadness, or fear, is a feeling that requires intimacy for its expression. A sensation of vulnerability often lies just beneath our anger, and we usually choose to show our vulnerability only to those we love because they are the ones we trust. Seen this way, expressing anger can be an intimate form of communication.

IT'S OUR CHOICE

Most newcomers to a Twelve Step program have rarely, if ever, dealt with anger soberly. Some people who were raised in alcoholic families never learned healthy ways either. If we did, we quickly lost this ability when alcohol or other drugs poisoned our responses. We became the "I want what I want when I want it" person. With this childish outlook, we believe we are king or queen of the day, and any obstacle to our gratification is met with an angry reaction. We will rarely, if ever, choose to respond to those feelings. We have so little control over their expression that they, not we, dictate our responses. We are driven impulsively and are often out of control. The feelings we have, although denied, are often expressed without any appropriate considerations.

Any expression of feeling in this immature, emotional state is a reaction, not a choice resulting from an awareness of feeling. When anger is a choice, simply airing the problems relieves tension. Anger becomes, then, a chosen response rather than a reaction to a situation or person; it is warm and caring, and does not coldly blame or ridicule the other person. We then take full responsibility for our feelings and don't accuse the other of "making us angry." When we choose to express anger, we reveal to others where we are most vulnerable.

Even when others don't respond favorably to us, we still increase our self-esteem and learn more of who we are.

If we choose to deny our anger, we temporarily avoid having to face anyone directly. Denial allows us to escape being vulnerable; it's a defense. However, the price we pay for this choice is a big one. Consistent denial of anger inevitably isolates us from intimate communication with others. Remember, denial of anger directly affects other feelings. Sadness, hurt, even happiness, become increasingly more difficult to feel. Denial of anger also develops resentments, and this can endanger our sobriety. For an alcoholic, this can mean death. Little wonder why we should be concerned about anger. Suppressed anger increases frustration and makes problem solving nearly impossible. Suppressed anger is at the root of many physical illnesses, divorce, child abuse, violence, anxiety, and various forms of mental illness. Even a mild case of suppressed anger can ruin our entire day. Sometimes, rather than face our feeling, we will try to explain or justify it. This dubious luxury, called "self-righteous anger," can also drive us back to our old, sick behaviors.

Nothing can be more damaging than "justified" anger. We are "playing God" when, in our justified anger, we contemplate revenge. Self-pity can become a constant companion, and the voice of this hellish companion blames, pouts, criticizes, accuses, and judges. In truth, we do not justify our anger, only what we have done with it. Deep in our hearts, we know how spiritually unhealthy this is and we try to justify it with statements like "I have a right to be angry with you." Feelings only need "rights" when we deny them. We can deny our feelings; it's our choice, but is it worth the price we pay?

COLD ANGER

Many of us, having denied our anger for years, return emotionally to deal with what is sometimes called *cold anger*. Cold anger, simply stated, is resentment. When we suppress our anger, the feeling seems to dissipate at first but, in truth, it turns cold and far more calculating. We begin to plot our responses (actually, our reactions) toward the person with whom we are angry. We grow more preoccupied with this person in our thoughts. With cold anger, even when we are active in a sport, at work, or simply taking a walk, we may find ourselves obsessively thinking about what was done or said to us. We are far from enjoying whatever we are doing. We are trapped in the past and plotting future revenge. This type of activity—"stewing"—is cooking serious trouble. This process, unchecked, will swell to a full-blown resentment. Remember, anger is only a feeling. But how we deal or don't deal with it may create a character defect. In the past, alcohol or other drugs, eating, sleeping, and headaches were often our responses to situations that frustrated us. We blamed others or pitied ourselves until we were blue in the face and choking with resentment. If our anger has turned cold and resentful, we may need to sit down with pencil and paper and write the name of the person we resent. Write down the particular incident. How were we affected? Did the person's behavior or remark affect our self-esteem, self-respect, security? Were we afraid or embarrassed? We may discover we are not angry, but hurt. After we identify what feeling may accompany our anger, we go to a mirror and rehearse discussing the problems with the other person. Very often tears may come to our eyes rather than anger. But if our anger does appear, this time we should express it and not let it sink into the cold realm of resentment. We can yell into the mirror, into the face we imagine has harmed us, shake our fists, whatever is necessary.

We can remind the imaginary face in the mirror that we do not want to blame him or her for our feelings, that we are trying to take responsibility for them. We only want to express how we feel. After this role playing, we may need to talk directly to the other person. Perhaps we should explain, in person, why we haven't called lately, why we have seemed so cold. Amends may be in order.

To avoid cold anger and resentment in the future, we need to learn how to express our anger warmly and immediately.

STOP, LOOK, AND LISTEN

Let's imagine ourselves driving to an appointment for a job interview or to meet a friend for lunch. Maybe we are driving to an AA or Al-Anon meeting; it only matters that it is important to arrive on time. We may even be a little late already. As we turn the corner onto a main street, we see a train crossing up ahead. As we stop at the crossing gate, we see we are the only ones waiting. Do we mumble under our breath? Can we no longer hear the song playing on the car radio? Perhaps the nice day now seems overcast. If this is happening, we are impulsively reacting and losing our ability to choose how we want to express our feelings.

One individual, in this very situation, noticed the railroad sign: Stop, Look, and Listen. He reinterpreted the advice on an emotional level and now uses the sign as a slogan. He stopped reacting to the situation over which he was powerless to change. He looked at how he felt and asked why he was so angry at the train and the delay. He listened for the answer.

When we find ourselves in similar situations we must *stop* reacting and *look* at how we feel. Are we afraid our tardiness might harm our chances for the job? Are we anxious about meeting our friend? Will that friend think less of us? We should ask what we are feeling right now, or why we are angry at the train. *Listen* to the response. This can be very difficult to do, but listening to what our hearts tell us is the healthiest way. The man found his slogan helped him not to react, but to choose a healthy way of responding *with* his feelings, not against them.

Now let's sit quietly in the car and watch the train. Earlier we took an inventory, and now we recall this very situation often provoked anger in us. Let's remind ourselves that to feel angry is not wrong. Remember, too, the train hasn't arrived intentionally to delay us, and *it* doesn't make us angry. If we realize this, we may take the opportunity now to see that this delay has actually helped us discover how important the job interview or friend is to us.

Discovering these things about ourselves while waiting for the train to pass increases our self-esteem. We now hear the song playing on the car radio once again. The blue in the sky returns. We now have more to offer whomever we meet.

ANGER AND HURT

Often other feelings can accompany our anger. We sometimes hear someone ask, "What's underneath the anger?" In this question, anger sounds like a disguise covering up something, perhaps another feeling. Usually, it's just accompanying another feeling. We can, and often do, feel anger and hurt simultaneously. Some people will find one or the other more difficult to express.

When we are angry and we stop, look, and listen, we'll often discover our vulnerability to pain alongside our anger. Someone in AA once said, "Whenever I'm angry, I know that often I'm also feeling hurt." We may not know what we are hurt about or even be able to express the hurt. All we may know is that we are upset and angry. Then, it will help to tell the person we're angry with, "Yes, I'm angry and yelling, but I know I'm hurt, too. I just can't seem to express hurt without yelling." We can then excuse ourselves to find some quiet time for meditation. We'll be amazed to find our anger has subsided, and in this atmosphere our hurt may surface. When we are hurt, we are most childlike and vulnerable. It takes courage to allow another person to see us this way. The choice, then, is ours. We can now go back to the person and make our feelings clearer.

When we find ourselves angry, we can ask ourselves these questions: Am I angry *and* hurt? Am I reacting to my hurt, my vulnerability, with anger? If I feel hurt also, have I made this clear to the other person, or has he or she only heard my anger? Am I reacting? Do I need a time-out? Any one of these questions can help us focus more clearly on what we are feeling.

ANGER IS A FEELING

There may be plenty of yelling in an alcoholic household, but the yelling doesn't express anger openly, warmly, or with resolve. Alcoholism is a family problem, and denial of alcoholism in the family is the major obstacle to recovery. Often, the feelings of each individual member of the family are also denied. They deny not only their own feelings but also those of others in the family. In fact, feelings are taboo.

We know now that feelings, in truth, are often responses to others. When honest, they are visible and apparent. In a family where denial of a serious illness is all-important, any genuine expression of feeling, and this includes anger, is generally denied by each member of the family. Honest feeling threatens to approach the problems. Little wonder, then, why alcoholic families deny feelings. Those raised in alcoholic families who marry or become alcoholics themselves need to go back to what Bill W. calls the "kindergarten of the spirit."

Many people feel it is wrong to be angry. Strangely enough, feelings like sadness or happiness are not considered wrong, yet anger is. We must repeat that anger is a feeling, a normal feeling that every human being on this earth has. What we do with our anger can cause serious emotional difficulties. If our anger isn't expressed and released, it goes back inside to wound us. Suppressed anger nurses resentment and self-pity, which can be fatal to a recovering alcoholic. Suppressed anger = pity = resentment = DRINK. We must keep this formula in mind.

Feelings are an adventure, something to explore rather than suppress. We are striving for wholeness, and wholeness is neither right nor wrong, but a state of being where we are most alive and conscious. Wholeness doesn't exclude anger or fear any more than it excludes happiness and sadness. Our feelings put us in touch with reality and other people; they allow intimacy between two people. Through our feelings we have the capacity to live joyfully and consciously. Mental health is expression of all our feelings. Anger is a friend in our hearts reminding us what we like, what we want, what we need. Let's stop, look, and listen to this friend.

We know how denial of anger causes blaming, aggression, and resentment. We know how seriously affected we are, physically, mentally, and spiritually, by denial of our anger. Our sobriety is at stake.

We can choose to continue denying our anger and allow ourselves to be driven impulsively into severe reactions and resentments, or we can choose to practice the principles of the Twelve Steps to help us better express our feelings. We can rehearse, before a mirror, what we feel, what we want to say to someone we're angry with. We can coin our own slogans to help us stop for a moment and consider carefully what we feel and how we want to express it. We know other feelings often accompany our anger. Anger doesn't mask these feelings, but merely accompanies them. We can, once again, accept anger as a feeling, not a character defect. In fact, we understand now that anger and our other feelings are friends, not enemies, that help make clearer to ourselves and others who we really are. The more we accept and are aware of anger, the more loving and caring our own lives become.

Hazelden Classics for Clients

In the past and present century alike, Hazelden has published the best known, most widely used literature that millions in recovery worldwide turn to for help, solace, and inspiration. Read by those from all backgrounds, our venerable "classic" pamphlets, written in words that echo the Twelve Step slogan "keep it simple," cover the challenges most often faced by generations on the "Road of Happy Destiny."

"No, I'm not angry!"

Releasing Anger assures readers that anger is a normal, even a healthy, feeling. Often enough, we deny we are angry. This behavior can lead to denying all of our feelings, which endangers sobriety. *Releasing Anger* helps us learn to become aware of our anger and get in touch with our feelings through use of the Twelve Steps. We can make the expression of anger a positive choice, not a negative reaction. In reading these pages, we'll discover that our feelings are something not to suppress but to explore.

Pamphlets in the Hazelden Classics for Clients series

It's Not As Bad As You Think
King Baby
Letting Go of the Need to Control
Queen Baby
Releasing Anger
Stinking Thinking

HAZELDEN®

www.hazelden.org
800-328-9000

Order No. 1420

ISBN 978-0-89486-249-6

90000

9 780894 862496